Planet Earth

EARLY LIFE ON EARTH

MICHAEL BRIGHT

PowerKiDS press

Published in 2018 by **The Rosen Publishing Group, Inc.**
29 East 21st Street, New York, NY 10010

Cataloging-in-Publication Data
Names: Bright, Michael.
Title: Early life on Earth / Michael Bright.
Description: New York : PowerKids Press, 2018. | Series: Planet Earth | Includes index.
Identifiers: ISBN 9781508153979 (pbk.) | ISBN 9781508153917 (library bound) | ISBN 9781508153801 (6 pack)
Subjects: LCSH: Evolution (Biology)--Juvenile literature. | Fossils -- Juvenile literature.
Classification: LCC QH367.1 B69 2018 | DDC 576.8--dc23

Written by Michael Bright
Cover illustration by Mark Turner
Editor: Corinne Lucas
Designer: Grant Kempster

Picture credits: p 4 © RICHARD BIZLEY/SCIENCE PHOTO LIBRARY; p 5 (tl) © Kris Wiktor/Shutterstock; p5 (tr) © Aleksandrs Jemeljanovs/Dreamstime; p 5 (m) © NOAA; p 5 (b) © NASA/JPL/CAL TECH; p 6 (r) © STEVE GSCHMEISSNER/SCIENCE PHOTO LIBRARY; p 6 (l) © Sergey/ CC Wikimedia Commons; p 7 (t) © Dr Ajay Kumar Singh/Shutterstock; p 7 (b) © Rob Bayer/ Shutterstock; p 8 (t) © Frank Fox/CC Wikimedia Commons; p 8 (b) Courtesy of Stefan Seibert, Brown University; p 9 (l) © RICHARD BIZLEY/SCIENCE PHOTO LIBRARY; p 9 (r) © Chen Junyuan; p 11 (m) RICHARD BIZLEY/SCIENCE PHOTO LIBRARY; p 11 (t) © Chase Studio/Science Source; p 11 (b)© Dinoton/Shutterstock; p 12 (t) © Bill Parsons/ Deviant Art; p 12 (b) © Obsidian Soul & Dimitriis Siskolpoulos/ CC Wikimedia Commons; p 13 (t) © Quade Paul/NSF; p 13 (m) © Universal Images Group North America LLC/DeAgostini/Alamy Stock Photo; p 13 (b) © AuntSpray/Shutterstock; p 14 © Dr. Morley Read/Shutterstock; p 15 (t) © Anton Handlirsch/ CC Wikimedia Commons; p 15 (m) © Catmando/Shutterstock; p 15 (b) © Lukaves/Dreamstime; p 16 (t) © R Aiden Martin/ Reef Quest Center for Shark Research; p 16 (b) © JAIME CHIRINOS/SCIENCE PHOTO LIBRARY; p 17 (t) © JAIME CHIRINOS/SCIENCE PHOTO LIBRARY; p 17 (b) © CHRISTIAN DARKIN/SCIENCE PHOTO LIBRARY; p 18 © RICHARD BIZLEY/SCIENCE PHOTO LIBRARY; p 19 (t) © WALTER MYERS/SCIENCE PHOTO LIBRARY; 19 (m) © Juan Gaertner/Shutterstock; p 19 (b) © GARY HINCKS/SCIENCE PHOTO LIBRARY; p 20 (t) © Dr Gunter Beckly/ CC Wikimedia Commons; p 20 (b) © Linda Bucklin/Shutterstock; p 21 (tl) © University of Edinburgh/PAI; p 21 (tr) © Smokeybjb/CC Wikimedia Commons; p 21 (bl) © DiBgd/CC Wikimedia Commons; p 21 (br) © Nobu Tamura/CC Wikimedia Commons; p 22 (t) © Ciavetti 2002; p 22 (b) © Linda Bucklin/Shutterstock; p 23 (t) © STEFAN SCHIESSL/SCIENCE PHOTO LIBRARY; p 23 © DiBgd/CC Wikimedia Commons; p 24 (t) © CHRISTIAN DARKIN/SCIENCE PHOTO LIBRARY; p 24 (b) © MAURICIO ANTON/SCIENCE PHOTO LIBRARY; p 25 (t) © WALTER MYERS/SCIENCE PHOTO LIBRARY; p 25 (b) © dmitrchel@mail.ru/CC Wikimedia Commons; p 26 (t) © DiBgd/CC Wikimedia Commons; p 26 (bl) © Dee Golden/Shutterstock; p 26 (br) © Maciej Bledowski/Shutterstock; p 27 (t) © Nobu Tamura/CC Wikimedia Commons; p 27 (m) © Mojcaj/CC Wikimedia Commons; p 27 (bl) © kurt_G/Shutterstock; p 27 (br) © popular business/Shutterstock; p 28 © Fotos593/Shutterstock; p 29 (t) © David Dales/Dreamstime; p 29 (b) © Dmitry Bogdanov/CC Wikimedia Commons. Background images and other graphic elements courtesy of Shutterstock.com.

Manufactured in China
CPSIA Compliance Information: Batch #BS17PK: For Further Information contact Rosen Publishing, New York, New York at 1-800-237-9932.

contents

ORIGINS
of life

Shortly after the formation of Earth 4.6 **billion** years ago, liquid water was thought to have collected on our planet's surface and life may have appeared as early as four billion years ago. However, despite this kind of scientific guesswork, the origins of life are covered in mystery, for exactly when, where and how it happened is far from clear …

from chemicals to cells

The basic chemicals of life either dropped on to Earth on **meteorites** from space, or they originated here. Lightning, ultraviolet light from the Sun, or heat from inside Earth changed them over time to make more complex chemicals. This was chemical **evolution**, and those chemicals were the **forerunners** of life's **molecules**. At some point they made copies of themselves and also gathered together to form cells, and each cell was surrounded by a wall. The cell was also able to copy itself, and so life began. This was the start of biological evolution.

The landscape of early Earth.

INVASION FROM SPACE

Life may not have started on Earth. Some of the complex chemicals that make up living things have been found all over the universe, so it is possible that life developed in any place where the conditions were right, including on our neighbor, Mars. Tiny living things then arrived on Earth as well-protected survival capsules called **spores**. They came to Earth on asteroids, comets, or meteorites. Scientists call this theory **panspermia**.

cauldrons of life

Where life started is another mystery. Here are just a few places on Earth where it might have begun.

In hot springs, volcanic pools and **geysers**, which are heated by **molten** rock below the Earth's surface.

In deep-sea vents or **fissures** on the floor of the deep sea, which squirt out very hot water and **minerals**. They are known as hydrothermal vents.

The early ocean was a **primordial soup** that contained some of the ingredients for life. Energy from lightning or ultraviolet light from the Sun could have turned those chemicals into more complex ones that eventually led to living things.

FIRST LIFE

The first living things were probably very simple, single cells. They would have been similar to **bacteria**-like **organisms** that are alive today. They are found in hot springs and deep-sea vents, the sorts of places where life might have started.

survival of the fittest

After the first cells had established themselves, new life-forms began to appear on Earth. They had gained an advantage over previous cells, because they could live in extreme conditions like those found on the early Earth. This made them slightly better and more able to survive. Scientists call this process evolution.

Archaea look like bacteria but are different.

Blue-green algae sometimes form lines or filaments.

blue-green bacteria

The earliest life-forms fed on chemicals in their environment, but then a life-form appeared that could make its own food using the gas carbon dioxide. This gas was found in the **atmosphere**. Carbon dioxide, water, and the energy from sunlight are needed for a process called **photosynthesis**, and some of the first organisms to use it were blue-green algae, a type of bacterium that still exists today.

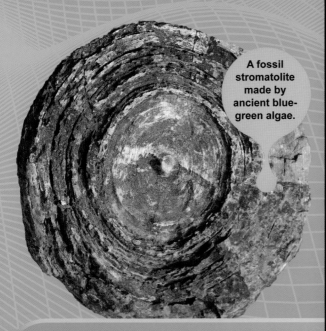

A fossil stromatolite made by ancient blue-green algae.

earliest signs of life

There are **traces** of life in crystals that are four billion years old, but the oldest recognizable forms of life are 3.48 billion years old and were found in Western Australia. They resemble the modern stromatolites, which look like cushion-shaped mats and are found in warm, shallow bays in Western Australia.

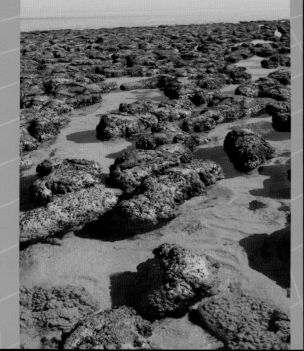

GEOLOGICAL TIME

Scientists divide the 4.6 billion years since Earth formed up to the present day into geological eons, eras, periods, epochs, and ages. This table shows the main ones. Figures are in millions of years, except for the Holocene.

Eon	Era	Period	Epoch
Phanerozoic (541 to present)	Cenozoic (65.5 to present)	Quaternary (2.588 to present)	
			Holocene (11,700 years to present) Pleistocene 2.58 mya to 11,700 years)
		Neogene (23.03 to 2.58)	Pliocene (5.333 to 2.58) Miocene (23.03 to 5.333)
		Paleogene (66 to 23.03)	Oligocene (33.9 to 23.03) Eocene (56 to 33.9) Paleocene (66 to 56)
	Mesozoic (251 to 65.5)	Cretaceous (145 to 66)	
		Jurassic (201.3 to 145)	
		Triassic (252.17 to 201.3)	
	Paleozoic (541 to 251)	Permian (298.9 to 252.17)	
		Carboniferous (358.9 to 298.9)	
		Devonian (419.2 to 358.9)	
		Silurian (443.8 to 419.2)	
		Ordovician (485.4 to 443.8)	
		Cambrian (541 to 485.4)	
Precambrian (4600 to 541)	Proterozoic (2500 to 541)		Ediacaran (635 to 541)
	Archean (4000 to 2500)		
	Hadean (4600 to 4000)		

first
ANIMALS

Scientists are cautious about describing the "first animal" because fossils are rare and identifying them is difficult. Living things that probably evolved from single-celled into multi-celled organisms could have made an appearance 1.5 billion years ago.

Modern Volvox colonies.

great-great-great-great-great... grandmother

The earliest multi-celled organism could have been a sphere of cells, similar in shape to the green alga Volvox. From this, flatter creatures evolved with a top and bottom. They had at least two layers of cells and were similar to the modern Trichoplax, a small, flattened but shapeless animal about less than an inch (1 mm) across. These flat animals were possibly the **ancestors** of all animals, including us.

first jellies

While sponges have traditionally been thought of as one of the first groups of animals to evolve, there is evidence to suggest that comb jellies may have beaten them to it. These would have been quite complex creatures, with a **nervous system**, unlike the sponges that have no nerves.

A comb jelly.

animals like plants

Hundreds of types of animals suddenly appeared during the Ediacaran period, which occurred 635–451 million years ago (mya). Scientists call it the "Avalon Explosion." Most of the animals were soft-bodied and in the shape of discs, tubes, or ferns and they stood or lay on the seabed.

One group was named the rangeomorphs. They were soft-bodied, fern-shaped creatures, up to 24 inches (60 cm) high. They lived in the deep sea, where they took in food directly from seawater through the surface of their body. Few other creatures were gobbling up the food, so they had it all to themselves.

Kimberella used its tube-like **proboscis** to feed on mats of bacteria.

LEFT AND RIGHT

The first animal with a head and left and right sides — known as bilateral symmetry — appeared during the Ediacaran period. It was worm-like and scientists gave it the tongue-twisting name Vernanimalcula.

9

cambrian EXPLOSION

All the major groups of animals in the world today appeared during the Cambrian period (541–485 mya). It was a time when animals began to develop weapons and defenses. It meant that some became **predators** and others their **prey**.

top predators

The most aggressive animal of this period was undoubtedly *Anomalocaris*. It was up to 6.6 feet (2 m) long and had a pair of arms, like shrimp tails, that grabbed its prey. On the underside of its head, its mouth had a ring of sharp teeth. Along its body were swimming flaps, so it must have been fast. It belonged to a group of animals known as **arthropods**, which are jointed-legged animals that include modern lobsters, insects, and spiders.

Anomalocaris had one of the first formidable weapons.

Opabinia had lobes along its body and a fan-shaped tail.

tube sucker

One of the strangest creatures was *Opabinia*. It had a long, flexible proboscis, like a miniature elephant's trunk, but with grasping spines at its tip. *Opabinia* probably thrust this down burrows to grab any worms hiding inside. Its body was up to 3 inches (8 cm) long. It might have been a **primitive** crustacean, related to shrimps and crabs.

Trilobites have three main body parts: head shield, body, and tail shield.

TRILOBITES

These easy-to-recognize arthropods resembled modern woodlice or pill bugs. Some fed on the seabed, while others were free-swimming and fed on tiny living things floating in the water, called **plankton.** The biggest individuals reached 28 inches (70 cm) in length during the *Ordovician* period (485.4–443.8 mya), and they were probably the most successful group of early animals. They existed for 270 million years, but they had died out by the end of the Permian period (252 mya).

The spines are covered with tiny triangular "scales."

spiky worms

Another oddball was *Hallucigenia*. It had tentacles with claws underneath its body for walking, and on its back were two rows of spines for protection. It was probably related to modern velvet worms, which are basically worms with legs.

armored slug

Wiwaxia was an oval-shaped, slug-like animal with hard scales covering its sides and two rows of spines on its back. It was up to 2 inches (5 cm) long and probably fed on mud on the seabed.

an age of FISH

The first animals with backbones, or vertebrates, were fish. They appeared during the Cambrian period (530 mya), but the real giants did not rule the seas until the Devonian period, about 150 million years later.

Conodont teeth either grasped and crushed prey or filtered the seawater.

Early fish-like Animals

The first fish-like creatures had a stiff rod called a notochord, rather than a backbone, running the length of their body. Some of the earliest were the conodonts. They were eel-like animals with hard teeth shaped like cones and combs, large eyes, chevron-shaped muscles, fins with fin rays and a notochord. They were 0.4–16 inches (1–40 cm) long, depending on the species.

first fish

Several fossil fish compete for the title of "first fish," *Pikaia* being one of them. It was shaped like a leaf, with a pair of head tentacles but no eyes, and resembled a modern lancelet. Its body was made up of rows of muscle blocks that pushed the animal along in S-shaped waves, like an eel.

Pikaia was 2 in (5 cm) long.

fish without jaws

Jawless armored fish had protective plates around their heads. They had eyes, breathed with **gills**, and fed by sucking prey into their jawless mouths. Fish with jaws evolved from one of these species.

fish with jaws

The first fish with jaws and teeth were the placoderms. They were heavily armored and most were predators. The largest known was *Dunkleosteus*, which lived about 360 mya. It was up to 36 feet (11 m) long (the length of a double-decker bus) and is thought to have been the world's first super-predator.

WATER MONSTERS

The early fish had to watch out for some of the largest arthropods that ever lived. They were sea scorpions known as euryptids, and the biggest type lived about 390 mya. It was 8 feet (2.5 m) long, with 18-inch (46 cm) claws. Sea scorpions were not true scorpions and many lived in freshwater, but they were one of the first really big predators on Earth.

INVASION
of the land

Life moved from the water onto the land in several stages. Carpets of algae were first, followed by simple plants. Close behind were insects and scorpions, and later came animals with backbones. Apart from everyday things, such as finding food and avoiding being eaten, the land presented new challenges. Animals had to get oxygen from the air rather than from water, and there was the risk of drying out.

first plants

About 450 mya, during the Ordovician period, the first plants made it onto the land. They had evolved from green algae living in shallow freshwater pools that probably dried up each summer. Only fossil spores have been found, but they indicate these pioneering plants were similar to modern leaf-like liverworts. Most avoided drying out by living in dark, damp places.

A modern leaf-shaped liverwort.

first insects

The oldest known insect fossil was found in Scotland and is 400 million years old. The insect had wings and was able to fly, so there must be even older fossils of insects without wings that we haven't found yet. They probably evolved from amphibious, hard-bodied, segmented creatures and developed a system of tubes to carry oxygen around the body so they could breathe in the air.

Insects evolved from aquatic ancestors, like this *Euthycarcinus*.

Coelacanths have leg-like fins.

OLD FOUR LEGS

Coelacanths were lobe-finned fish that evolved about 425 mya, and surprisingly, two species are still alive today: one in the western Indian Ocean and one off Indonesia. They have changed very little in all that time, so they are known as "living fossils."

a leg on each corner

The lobe-finned fish were similar to modern lungfish. They gave rise to the first **amphibians** — animals with backbones that spend part of their lives in water and part on land, such as frogs and salamanders.

Their fleshy fins turned into legs to walk on land, and their **swim bladders** evolved into lungs so they could breathe in the air.

An animal that shows this **transition** is *Tiktaalik*, which lived 375 mya during the Devonian period. It looked similar to a crocodile, but it had fins like a fish.

385
mya

375
mya

365
mya

first SHARKS

About 450 mya, fish split into two main groups. One group had rigid bony skeletons, like modern salmon, and the other had skeletons made of bendy cartilage, like modern sharks and rays. Many of the early sharks had streamlined, torpedo-shaped bodies, so they could swim fast. It seems sharks were successful ocean predators right from the start.

first shark-like fish

The spiny sharks lived at the beginning of the Silurian period (443.8–419.2 mya), but they were not like modern sharks. They had the same cartilage skeleton, but were covered with scales like modern gars and bowfins, which are bony fish.

few fossils

Sharks have left few clues about what they were like because their skeletons are made of soft, bendy cartilage which does not fossilize as well as bone. Most evidence comes from their teeth and body scales. The earliest scales are 420 million years old and come from a shark called *Elegestolepis*. The earliest teeth are 400 million years old and from a *Leonodus* shark, but nobody knows what either looked like.

primitive shark

One of the earliest recognizable sharks was *Cladoselache*. It was 6.6 feet (2 m) long, streamlined, and had stiff triangular fins. Fossilized fish remains found tail first in its stomach indicate it was a fast-swimming predator that could catch up with its prey. It lived about 370 mya.

Cladoselache had 5–7 gill slits.

freshwater sharks

The shark *Xenacanthus* lived in freshwater about 280 mya. It was an eel-shaped shark, about 3.3 feet (1 m) long, with a very long spine on the back of its head. The dorsal fin on its back ran the length of its back and around its tail, like a modern conger eel.

GOLDEN AGE OF SHARKS

During the Carboniferous period, sharks and their relatives took on some bizarre shapes. The strangest must have been *Helicoprion*, which had a **whorl** of teeth in its lower jaws that resembled a circular saw. Another oddball was the *Stethacanthus*. Male sharks of this type had structures that looked like spiky stools on their backs.

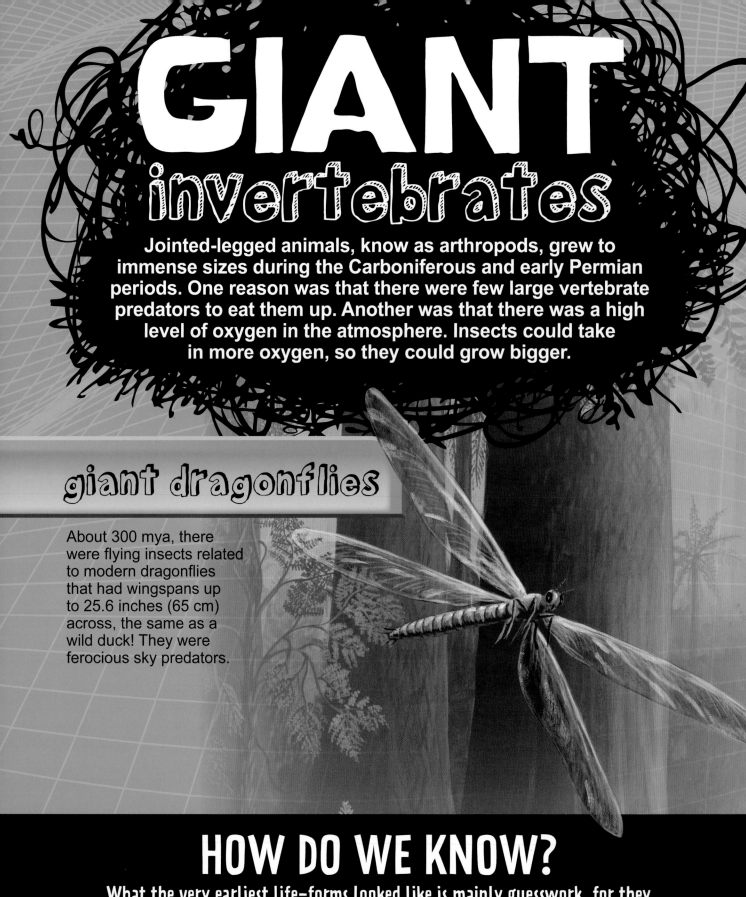

GIANT
invertebrates

Jointed-legged animals, know as arthropods, grew to immense sizes during the Carboniferous and early Permian periods. One reason was that there were few large vertebrate predators to eat them up. Another was that there was a high level of oxygen in the atmosphere. Insects could take in more oxygen, so they could grow bigger.

giant dragonflies

About 300 mya, there were flying insects related to modern dragonflies that had wingspans up to 25.6 inches (65 cm) across, the same as a wild duck! They were ferocious sky predators.

HOW DO WE KNOW?

What the very earliest life-forms looked like is mainly guesswork, for they were made of soft parts that do not preserve well. For the rest, scientists rely on finding fossils in rocks. When a living thing dies and **sediments** cover it, the chemicals in its body are replaced by minerals from the rock. It is literally turned to stone or, in the case of the swamp forests, into coal.

giant millipedes

Imagine a millipede 8.5 feet (2.3 m) long! This was the length of the plant-eating *Arthropleura*. Fossilized footprints, consisting of long, side-by-side rows of tiny footprints, show how this enormous millipede must have moved quickly through the forest. It was the world's largest known land invertebrate.

coal forests

The giant invertebrates lived in thick rainforests and swamp forests. The climate was tropical, the air was moist, and the trees were tall. The *Lepidodendron* grew 100 feet (30 m) tall! This giant is related to modern quillworts, which are small plants with long hollow shafts for leaves. There were tree ferns and seed ferns, and a variety of low-growing plants. All of the trees and plants are thought to have pumped large amounts of oxygen into the air, up to 35%, compared to 21% today. Then, about 305 mya, the vegetation began to die down and sediments covered the remains. The plants were turned into coal.

The tree is buried in sediment before it decays.

Minerals replace the tree's tissues.

Soft rocks erode away, leaving the stone fossil tree.

A tree dies.

AMPHIBIANS
rule

For tens of millions of years, during the Carboniferous and early Permian periods, the dominant animals on Earth were amphibians. Some were small with thin, moist skin like today's frogs and salamanders, while others were big reptile-like monsters.

leaving the pond

One pre-amphibian four-legged vertebrate was called the *Acanthostega*. It was one of the first to have legs, fingers, and toes rather than fins. It couldn't walk too well so it probably waded through shallow swamps, grabbing and eating invertebrate prey at the water's edge.

Two long bones supported *Diplocaulus*'s head.

triangular head

Another pre-amphibian creature was the *Diplocaulus*. It had a salamander-shaped body, about 3.3 feet (1 m) long, and a large, boomerang-shaped head. This would have made it hard for predators to swallow and would help it steer through water.

hide from the sun

The 10-foot-long (3 m) *Metoposaurus* lived at a time when the climate alternated regularly between wet and dry. It survived droughts by digging a burrow with its broad, flat head and wide hands and hiding away. During the wet seasons, it hunted in lakes.

big head

One of the heaviest amphibians was the 10-foot-long (3 m) *Diadectes*. It had a massive head, like a hippo, and was one of the first amphibians to be an exclusive plant eater.

reptile-like amphibians

Many of the prehistoric amphibians had the shape of modern crocodiles. The *Eogrinus* was a slender beast, with scaly rather than moist skin. At 15 feet (4.6 m) long, it was one of the longer amphibians at the time. The *Eryops* was shorter at 6 feet (2 m) long, but sturdily built with massive, teeth-filled jaws and stocky, **splayed** legs.

MODERN AMPHIBIANS

The 8-inch-long (20 cm) *Amphibamus* is possibly the ancestor of all modern amphibians: frogs, toads, salamanders, newts, and earthworm-like caecilians.

monster amphibians

Like all major predatory groups, the amphibians had their monsters. The *Mastodonsaurus* had a gigantic, flattened head like a crocodile that took up the first third of its 20-foot-long (6 m) body. It was one of the largest amphibians ever to have lived.

the first REPTILES

The earliest known reptiles lived in the rainforests during the late Carboniferous period, before the climate became drier. They were more suited to living on land than the amphibians. A key advance was the reptile egg. Amphibians laid their eggs in water, but reptile eggs contained water inside the egg so the baby reptile could develop safely on land.

reptile pioneer

One of the earliest known reptiles was the *Hylonomus*. It was a small, lizard-like animal about 8 inches (20 cm) long that scampered about in the rainforest, avoiding the giant amphibians. It had tiny sharp teeth, and ate small insects.

Mesosaurus's teeth turn outwards.

RETURN TO THE SEA

With giant amphibians disappearing, a few early reptiles returned to the water. The *Mesosaurus* had a 3.3-foot-long (1 m), streamlined body, and webbed feet. It propelled itself along with its long hind legs. It fed on shrimp-like creatures, and was probably a forerunner of the giant marine reptiles that later shared the planet with the dinosaurs.

all change

About 305 mya, many of the world's rainforests collapsed and dry conditions spread across much of the single supercontinent, Pangaea. Deserts were widespread, which favored plants with seeds in a protective cover. The first modern trees — conifers, ginkgos, and cycads — replaced many of the spore-producing plants, such as *Lepidodendron*. These conditions gave the reptiles an advantage. They began to take over the places where the amphibians had previously lived.

new predators

The mammal-like reptiles became the dominant predators on Earth. The 15-foot-long (4.6 m) *Dimetrodon* is recognized by the enormous "sail" on its back. The sail's function is unknown, but it might have helped control the animal's temperature. *Dimetrodon* looked like a dinosaur, but was not one. It was one of a group that gave rise to the reptiles that eventually became mammals.

The sail was more than 3.3 ft (1 m) tall.

PREDATORS
vs prey

During the middle and late Permian period, several groups of very large reptile-like animals appeared. Some were big, stocky plant eaters, and others were strong and formidable predators. The plant eaters had heavy, thick skulls with bony bumps, and the predators had front teeth that interlocked.

giant predator

The meat-eating *Titanophoneus* had a massive skull with a long snout with interlocking front teeth. At up to 16 feet (5 m) long, it was one of the largest predators of its time, but its splayed legs indicate it was probably a bit slow. It ambushed its prey rather than running it down, killing its victim with a powerful bite to the neck.

Large canine teeth killed with a bite to the prey's neck.

heavy plant eater

Tapinocephalus was a plant eater with a huge barrel-shaped body and a massive bony roof to its skull, like a crash helmet. Males of the species probably engaged in head butting, like modern mountain sheep, to gain territory or a mate. *Tapinocephalus* was over 10 feet (3 m) long.

reptilian wolves

Lycosuchus and *Pristerognathus* were active predators that lived at the end of the Permian period, 265–245 mya. Both were about the size of a large dog, and *Lycosuchus* had two large canine teeth in each side of the upper jaw. Both beasts fed on small animals, perhaps hunting in packs like wolves.

EPIC BATTLES

Inostrancevia was part of a group of mammal-like reptiles that were **apex predators**, right at the top of their food chain. It was almost the size of a rhino, up to 11.5 feet (3.5 m) long, and had extra long canine teeth, which were 6 inches (15 cm) long, like a saber-toothed cat. It shared living space with the massive, plant-eating *Scutosaurus*. The **herbivore** was more than 10 feet (3 m) long and bulky, so it moved slowly. Its main defense was a skull sporting bony spikes and it had bony plates under its skin, like chain mail. No doubt predator and prey clashed often in the semi-deserts of the late Permian period.

Signs of the FUTURE

Towards the end of the Permian period, creatures were appearing that scientists recognize as the forerunners of modern animals, such as the mammals. They were reptilian, but they were beginning to show features that we would recognize today.

standing tall

Bunostegos, meaning "knobbly roof," was a cow-sized, plant-eating reptile with large bony knobs on and around its head. It was unusual in that it walked with its four limbs directly below its body, like a mammal, rather than splayed out to the side like a lizard. It was the first vertebrate with four legs to do so. It lived in a dry desert region in the center of the Pangaea supercontinent, about 260 mya.

PERMIAN WILDLIFE

In the sea there were plenty of coral reefs around the coast of Pangaea. In deeper water, ammonites were common. Most had spiral shells, like a snail. Bony fish were replacing those lobe-finned fish that came before the amphibians. Bugs, similar to the ones we have today, started to appear on land. They had needle-like mouthparts to pierce plant stems and suck out the sap. Cicadas and beetles also arrived during the Permian period (252–201 mya).

The cynodonts, meaning "dog teeth," were reptiles that were similar to mammals. The early species were relatively small and they appeared in the late Permian period. They had a second **palate** inside their mouth that allowed them to chew and breathe at the same time, speeding up digestion. Their predecessors swallowed everything whole without chewing. They had large heads like mammals, but their brains were small. They were nudging towards being warm-blooded and the smaller cynodonts might have had fur and whiskers.

Procynosochus was an early cynodont.

The *Procynosochus* had teeth with a working surface like a mammal's cheek teeth. It might have had a diaphragm like we have as well. This is the flat muscle that separates the heart and lungs from the stomach and intestines. *Procyonosochus* probably chewed its food rather than just swallowing it, and it may have hunted in lakes and rivers.

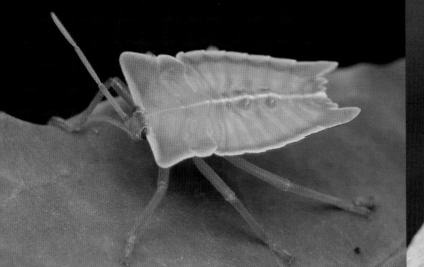

Charassognathus was a fierce predator.

the time of the
GREAT DYING

Life in the Permian period was brought to an abrupt end by the largest loss of plant and animal life in our planet's history. During this mass extinction, life on Earth almost disappeared completely. About 90% of all species were wiped out, especially those living in the sea. Only 4% survived and lived into the Triassic period (252.17–201.3 mya).

triple whammy

The cause of the mass extinction is unknown, but vast **lava fields** in northern Russia, known as the Siberian Traps, were probably involved in the mass extinction. They were formed by the largest volcanic eruptions in Earth's history, which lasted on and off for two million years. On top of that, it is likely that there was an impact from an asteroid. Scientists have found a 75-mile-wide (120 km) crater of the right age in Australia. It was made by an asteroid 3 miles (4.8 km) across. It would have smothered the world in billions of tons of debris, dust, poisonous gases, and **acid rain**. In addition, the oceans may have lost much of their oxygen at the time or turned acidic, making it difficult for life to survive. Altogether, these things made for a global catastrophe with very few survivors.

fungi heaven

Almost all of the world's trees disappeared during the mass extinction, but this was good news for fungi. The enormous quantities of dead wood meant the amount of fungi increased dramatically.

GREAT THINGS AHEAD

Amongst the survivors that made it through to the Triassic period were the archosaurs, meaning "ruling reptiles," and their odd-shaped relatives, including the hippo-sized, parrot-beaked *Hyperodapedon*, and the ultra-slim, long-necked *Prolacerta*. Had the archosaurs not survived, we would never have had the most famous group of prehistoric animals that ever lived . . . the dinosaurs.

triassic predators

The largest reptile to take over as apex predator after the mass extinction was the *Erythrosochus*. It had a stocky body, a large head on a short neck, and its powerful jaws were lined with sharp, conical teeth. Another large predator, which was similar to a modern crocodile, was the *Proterosochus*. It was probably an ambush predator that waited for animals to come to the water, much like a Nile crocodile.

glossary

acid rain rain containing high levels of dangerous chemicals that turn the water from neutral to acid

amphibian an animal with a backbone that lives partly in water and partly on land

ancestor an animal from which later animals evolved

apex predator a hunter at the top of the food chain

arthropod a hard-bodied, jointed-legged animal without a backbone

atmosphere the layer of gases around a planet

bacteria a group of single-celled living things, some of which cause diseases

billion a thousand million

evolution the gradual process by which something living changes into a better form

fissure a crack in rocks

forerunner something or someone who has gone before

geyser a natural hot spring that squirts boiling water into the air

gills organs used by fish for breathing underwater

herbivore an animal that eats plants

lava field a large area of molten volcanic rock that has cooled and become solid

meteorite a piece of rock or metal that has fallen onto Earth from space

minerals chemicals not made by plants or animals, which have been formed by a geological process

molecule the smallest part of a substance that can take part in a chemical reaction

molten hot and liquid

nervous system the network of nerve cells and fibers that carries electrical impulses from one part of the body to another

organism a living thing

palate the separation of the mouth and nose cavities in the roof of the mouth

panspermia the theory that life on Earth arose first somewhere in space

photosynthesis the process by which green plants and algae create sugars using carbon dioxide, water, and energy from the Sun

plankton tiny living things that float around in the sea

predator an animal that hunts and eats other animals

prey an animal that is eaten by another animal

primitive the early stage of something

primordial soup the name given to Earth's early ocean because it contained many of the ingredients needed to make life

proboscis nose-like structure

sediments tiny particles of rock that are carried by wind, water, or ice

splayed spread out to the sides

spore a seed-like form that a bacterium changes into so it can withstand bad conditions

swim bladder an air-filled sac inside a fish that helps it stay at the right depth in the water

trace tiny amount

transition a change from one thing to another

whorl a coiled shape

Books

Billions of Years, Amazing Changes: The Story of Evolution (2011)
Laurence Pringle
Boyds Mill Press

Evolution Revolution (2016)
Robert Winston
DK Children

Evolution: The Story of Life on Earth (2011)
Jay Hosler and Kevin Cannon
Hill and Wang

Evolution: The Whole Life on Earth Story (2014)
Glenn Murphy
Pan Macmillion

Life on Earth: The Story of Evolution (2002)
Steve Jenkins
HMH Books for Young Readers

Websites

PowerKids Press has developed an online list of websites related to the subject of this book. This site is updated regularly. Please use this link to access the list:
www.powerkidslinks.com/pe/earlylife

index